THE ONLY LIFE WORTH LIVING

REMOVING THE SENSE OF SEPARATION
RESTORING WHOLENESS

A BOOK OF SPIRITUAL PRACTICES

GERALD E. COLLINS

PublishAmerica
Baltimore

First printing

PublishAmerica has allowed this work to remain exactly as the author intended, verbatim, without editorial input.

This publication contains the opinions and ideas of its author. Author intends to offer information of a general nature. Any reliance on the information herein is at the reader's own discretion.

The author and publisher specifically disclaim all responsibility for any liability, loss, or right, personal or otherwise, which is incurred as a consequence, directly or indirectly, of the use and application of any contents of this book. They further make no representations or warranties with respect to the accuracy or completeness of the contents of this work and specifically disclaim all warranties including without limitation any implied warranty of fitness for a particular purpose. Any recommendations are made without any guarantee on the part of the author or the publisher.

ISBN: 1-60836-501-8
PUBLISHED BY PUBLISHAMERICA, LLLP
www.publishamerica.com
Baltimore

Printed in the United States of America

Table of Contents

Foreword

I met Gerald many years ago when were matriculating through one of the many classes we have taken at our spiritual center. Even then he was an ardent student of spiritual philosophy and its practice. His commitment to the study—and practice—of that philosophy is evident in this book.

Take your time with the words. Take your time with the practices. And when you rediscover the wholeness of which he speaks you will more fully understand and might I say appreciate the consciousness which he himself has become because of this work. Enjoy the book and enjoy the transformation it will inspire.

Peace and blessings,
Eugene Lovick

INTRODUCTION

The erroneous belief that you are separate from your creator is the cause of lack, loneliness, fear, depression, and illness. The purpose of this book is to heal this erroneous belief. Thus this book deals with true cause. It doesn't seek to satisfy ego desires that keep a person chasing the world of effects without success. Thus if you are looking for another spiritual development book that is to help you fix some ego need or promises a quick fix, this may not be the book for you. However, if you tire of the workshops, books, and processes that cause you to assume that you are broken in some way, this may be the right fit for you.

Spiritual growth, awakening, having a closer relationship with God, and growing in spiritual strength are all considered here. Healing the sense of separateness covers all of the above as it means the same thing.

Beloved child, you are a perfect creation of a most loving, generous, gentle, and just creator. You are not broken in any way. Now let me seek to show your why this is so.

Imagine at your creation you were given a plot of land. For your entire life all you have to do is take care of this plot. Nothing is near the importance of this task. It is the reason for your creation. There are some things you should know about your plot of land.

Of course with land the most important thing is location, location,

location. This is the common thought about real estate. Fortunately unlike most common thoughts, this one is true. The land you have been given is in the best location possible.

While location is the first, value is the second important thing about this plot of land. This land has immense value. You will be told later herein why this is of critical importance.

Third is the unlimited possibilities inherent with this plot of land. Unlimited possibilities means that this plot of land can become anything. This is not much different than item number two above. Yet it professes to infinite possibilities.

I submit to you that this plot of land is your spirit/mind. Its location is right where you are. Its value is very high or should be considered to be so because spirit/mind is all that you are. You are not a body. Nor is mind part of the body. Please do not confuse mind with the brain. The brain is part of the body. You are a state of awareness which is nothing more than spirit/mind. Since you are spirit/mind, you have unlimited possibilities. This is because as you become aware of your true nature you then learn that you can do anything.

Finally understand that mind is all that exist. There is only one mind. However, in order to join with one of the desires of your creator all of us have been given the task of taking care of mind. That is what we must do. If we just do that, world peace will result, hunger will be a thing of the past, and all (I do mean all) of the worlds problems will cease to exist as will your perceived problems.

However, none of us can cause others to accept this premise and begin to bring better care to their plot of land. Each of us must be willing to do it for ourselves.

Assume this mind to be like a pool of water. There is some dirt in the water which has caused a portion of the water to be less clear. One teaching calls this dirt race consciousness. Another calls it carnal mind. If you take on the task of cleaning up the mud in your mind it is like cleaning up a portion of the great pool of water which is the great mind. You can take on a greater task which is seeking to clean up minds of others. However, don't fool yourself. There is just one mind. Anyone or anything that comes into your awareness is just another aspect of your mind. Thus cleaning up the mind of a perceived other is actually cleaning up your own mind. Clean up your own mind and let the benefits flow. This keeps you from blaming others. More on this later herein.

To take this even deeper lets ask a question and follow a logical conclusion. Since there is just one mind and that mind is the mind of God, would God allow anyone to dirty the mind of God? The obvious answer is no! God would not allow anyone to dirty the mind of God. Therefore what we see as dirt in this pool of water is an illusion. We affirm the truth by learning to deny this illusion. In that way we clean the pool.

Your five senses were made just to assist you in navigating the world you appear to live in. The important thing is to understand that these five senses will seek to fool you continuously. You must learn to experience this differently. Never let yourself begin to believe anything other that the truth about yourself. There is just one mind and that mind is the mind of God. That mind is perfect as God created it. You are therefore perfect.

Some years ago one of my teachers told me to take my humanhood and write it on a sheet of paper. I was then to take this sheet of paper and burn it. I must admit that I never did what was suggested although I do recall the lesson. At the time of the lesson, I did agree with the statement. That teacher was trying to tell me something and cause me to do a process to help my recollection of that experience. In this book you will be given several processes. It is my prayer that you consider doing the processes this book suggest to help cement the lesson in your mind. Reading alone is not sufficient. You must also select some truths that you practice. Without prayer, practice and study, you stay in philosophy. It may also be helpful to begin to journal some of the truths that come to you during the reading and from your meditations. Yes, some stillness time is required.

Now we can make the statement again with the above factors supporting it. It is being made in the first person: "I am a perfect creation of a loving, generous, gentle, and just creator. I am the mind of God. I and my creator are one." You can only be one with your creator if you are a spirit. As a body you can see that the body has a location. As a spirit you have no specific location. As a spirit one with God you are everywhere like your creator.

God is just because God placed the most important thing about you right where you are. You do not need to seek outside your real being to find anything you need. God is generous because by the proper use of this mind you can create anything, thus it is obvious that you are the beloved of God and that God is a gentle being.

God is just because if you do not control your mind you will simply experience the effects of that mind. My five senses tell me of a world of scarcity, suffering, and problems. Simply put you can choose to believe these as truths of the world and you will experience those things. Or, you can begin the path of purifying your mind and begin to experience more of the blessings of a being who has joined with its creator to take attention off what newspapers, television, and other media as well as what the past experiences have reported.

Jesus made the following statement two thousand years ago: "Seek ye first the kingdom of God and its righteousness and all things shall be added.[1]"

The analogy of the plot of land and the care you must give it are all contained in the above statement. In other words, find the errors that you already have in your mind and do not add to them. Also note the word "first" in the above line. I suggest that this means that you should give some priority to the work of cleaning your mind. This writing will tell you how not to add to your existing mental errors later. Right now we return to the land allegory to assist understanding some things:

1. My land is in a perfect location. It is right where I am.

Bible Support:	The kingdom of God is within you[2]
Logical Suggestion:	God is right where you are.
Reason to accept belief:	Causes one to stop seeking outside the self for the God within.

2. My land is of immense value. Anything loved must be of value.

Bible Support:	"Love the lord God with all your might, love your neighbor as yourself….[3]"
Logical Suggestion:	You are loved and loveable.
Reason to accept belief:	Increases self love

3. My land has unlimited potential. There is power here.

Bible Support:	"You will be able to tell that mountain to fall and it will fall…[4]"

Logical Suggestion:	You are a being of power.
Reason to accept belief:	Accesses the unlimited power of God within

I came across a poem in which the writer says the following about God: "Closer is he than breathing, and nearer than hands and feet[11]." Doesn't this say it well. God is right where you are. You and God are one. Please understand that like God oneness is a spiritual concept and has no counterpart in the physical world.

This entire writing has at its base one purpose. It is to help you heal the sense of separation that you may have. Healing is the lie. The sense of separation is the truth. It is only a sense of separation. There is nothing that needs healing. An incorrect belief needs to be corrected. As you become more clear about your oneness and union in God your surroundings begin to take on the vibration of this higher belief system. The truth just announces itself by what appears in the outer as an improvement in circumstances. Just like light erases darkness. Truth corrects error.

Another way of saying this is that anytime you take a growth step there will be blessings. At minimum you will feel very good. It's like God becomes more good to you because you have done something good. This is not true although it appears to be so. Everything the eyes see is error. Doesn't matter whether they see good or something less that what appears to be good at that time. The body's eyes were not made to see the presence of God. Fortunately there is something within you that does know of this presence. Your eyes and my eyes were made to see the world of effects and keep you believing in separation. This is true of all five senses. Their purpose is to suggest something other than the natural love that you have for all creation and the natural love that all creation has for you. As you do the work of healing the sense of separation, that natural love that you are and a sense of peace will blossom within you.

Before going any further lets' summarize:

1. I am mind/spirit.

2. One of my purposes in life is to clean my mind/spirit. This means that I am to let go of my erroneous beliefs.

3. Since there is only one mind which is the mind of God, what appears as unclean is an illusion.

Item number three uses the word unclean. This is really a misnomer. Saying that something appearing as dirt is an illusion also means that all the things judged as good are not illusion. Unless you are well developed, your eyes see a large percentage of error and some aspect of reality. It is probably better to say that the five senses only suggest complete error. Otherwise one would be saying that one can judge all things that they experience at the time of the experience. Few can accurately do this. The suggestion is to call all things God. That is the truth. God is all there is and God is good.

Are You in Agreement?

It is entirely possible that you are not convinced. You may still desire or seek to see yourself as a body. Well that is ok. You have every right to believe what you want. This is being said in plain language and it has been said so plainly that you may not have thought of it this way. Yet something has brought you to this point to read these words. One of my teachers told me that when the student is ready the teacher shows up. You can choose to make these words one of your teachers or you may choose to continue reading with an open mind.

There is another reason for seeing yourself as a spirit. Everything in form eventually disintegrates. Seeing yourself as a spirit allows you to see the eternality of your existence. All bodies die as yours and mine will one day. However spirits are eternal. This helps you to eliminate your fear of death. Some believe that by being good that they will go to heaven and live forever. The only way to truly see your possibility of eternal existence is by seeing yourself as God created you. You are an eternal spirit.

You may also choose to believe that your basic function is to build a company, go on a major mission of mercy to fix a situation in the world, or something else that is big in the world of effects. That may be true. However, the premise on which this writing is based is that each person has dual purposes when taking apparent human form. Strengthening the belief in the power within can do nothing but assist in your ability to bring more power and faith to whatever you do in the outer world. How can anyone suggest that healing the sense of separation from God is not of value? Since this writing is based upon the belief of everyone having a mind has the ability to pollute the great pool of water (mind) that we all exist in, it is suggested that everyone join in the work of cleaning their area of the pool. Instead of using the allegory of the self as land, from this point forward we will consider our purpose as cleaning our area of the great pool of mind.

The Practice of the Presence of God

Anything that one desires to do well requires practice and attention. My first minister had a story he often told about a conductor of a major symphony named Peter who was walking down the street in New York. Someone walked up to Peter and asked him directions to get to

Carnegie Hall. Peter then responded saying: "Practice, Practice, and more Practice." If you desire to do anything well just begin to practice.

In the seventeenth century there was a monk who had taken on the job of cleaning the kitchen each day. This monk did not like this duty and decided that he would find a way to enjoy this duty. He decided to keep his mind on God all day to enjoy this being called God and do his duties. This monk who is named Brother Lawrence found that God is joy and anything done with God in mind becomes enjoyable. Brother Lawrence is credited with creating this practice called "Practicing the Presence of God." There are several writings on this topic. You can begin some research on it. However, you must practice this and become proficient at this practice. It will make all your activities enjoyable and you will become better at anything you do.

To do this you must imagine that you are always in the presence of God. Feel this presence and stay in the present moment to stay in this zone. Anything you do will then take on a flavor and feeling that is enriched with the God presence. Again this is something you must practice and become proficient at. This is probably the most important practice to be given you in this writing. Do it upon awakening and stay in the God presence. Do it now and continue reading. It requires that you be in this moment and sometimes you must feel the God presence as much as you can. There are many feelings that will arise through this practice and they cannot be assumed to be the same with each person. Just begin and let this happen. You will get guidance and find life more enjoyable. Note that the next chapter is actually devoted to some cognitive information on the practice. Remember that the practice of the principles is more important than reading them repeatedly. Practice means applying principles throughout your day in spite of what you are doing. Opportunities to practice will arise.

Living in a consistent state of joy is one aspect of the only life worth living. There are several others that this writing explains. Read on.

Using Scriptures

A few words about the common practice of writers who take select passages from scripture to support something they are saying. It doesn't matter whether these passages are taken from the Bible, the Holy Koran, or some other sacred text. Hundreds of religions have been created by people who have done this. All of these religions have statements of truth within them and all of them have error or misinterpretations within them. Holy books are interpreted differently by different people. The errors are only perceived. And it is accepted that anyone can take something out of a context and use it to support something they are saying. Truthfully, none of this really matters. All thought systems are paths to the God within. These thought systems or religions as they are often called actually put you on a path and hopefully, you later seek deepen the path you are already on. Just be aware that you are on a path returning to your maker. Also remember that this is done within the mind.

In other words, this writer loves and believes in the presence of God. Nothing said here can hurt you. Its intent is to help you become clear about what you really are. This writing is the result of my training as a Practitioner of Truth in Agape International Center for eleven years, teaching these concepts to children in stories and other simplified forms, over twenty years of meditation, having read an untold number of books, and numerous workshops and seminars attended. Its intention is only to assist you to believe in your wholeness. Therefore, that is all that it can do.

However, there are some things that the statements in this writing should do for you:

1. They should strengthen your faith in the God within. If you accept that God is right where you are instead of in heaven well away from you, this work should help you immensely.

2. They should move you toward fearlessness because if you are not a body nothing and no one can really hurt you.

3. They should also remove any fear you have regarding death because death is of a body. You are a spirit/mind that is eternal.

4. This writing will also take you through what is true creation and will therefore help you release things that you have created that no longer serve you.

How to Use this Book

Seven chapters of this book are written for you to use them as a daily work.

For example read the chapter on One Power on Sunday as the first day of the week. Read each of the succeeding chapters on the following days. Read only one chapter a day. If for any reason you miss a day. Just go on to the next day. Do not do two chapters any day. Do this for a period of about six weeks. At the end of this period you will be a different person. Actually you will be a different thought. You will be a more beautiful thought.

The first chapter is to be read on Sunday morning. If you are starting this book on another day, skip to the day of the week that has the practice for that day. For example, if you are starting the practice part of this book on Wednesday. Read the chapter that is headed up as the Wednesday Reading and Practice.

If you have not had experience with meditation this does not matter. Just close your eyes and bring your thoughts to what you are saying as instructed. This is really so easy that you really can only judge that you are not doing it well. You can do this. Don't judge, just do it. This is another of those erroneous thoughts. It may seem that you are not doing it while you may really be doing it very well.

You will also note an affirmation usually stated always in the first person for you to say to yourself each day. If for some reason after reading the chapter and you do not have the time for the meditations, just say the affirmation to yourself. Come back to the meditation when you are ready.

As you go through your day try to bring your attention to God every three hours. For example, assume you begin your day at six am. At this time you would read a chapter and do the meditation for that day. Thus at nine am, twelve noon, three pm, and six pm spend at least one minute in the awareness that you live within the presence of God. I for example use my cell phone to alert me every three hours. If I am unable to stop at the time that my cell phone alerts me, I just remember to come to a stop a little later. Give about one minute to this no less than four times today if you can remember. As you do the one minute meditations try to sense the presence of God in some way. At minimum seek to bring yourself to a complete stop for about a minute.

If you can, make the chapter reading and meditation one of the first task that you do upon awakening. Other times later in the day will also work. Just give yourself about twenty minutes to do the reading and meditation exercises. You may need a kitchen timer to enable you to give seven minutes to the meditation portion of your grounding exercise. By the way, it is ok to spend the entire seven minutes doing the contemplative meditation part of the meditation time. This means that you may repeat the words in your mind the entire seven minutes.

This may sound a little complicated at first. Believe me, it is not. Just read a chapter and do the meditation each day. Then every three hours ground yourself in the awareness of your oneness in God.

After completion of a week, read the last chapter of this book. If you simply desire reading, you may read the entire book and come back to the meditation exercises. The first and last chapters are book ends for the daily work that you are to do. You may read them repeatedly as well to assist understanding. Your life is eternal. Do this whatever way you desire. However, my purpose is to help move you to clarity and wholeness of mind/spirit as soon as possible. The exercises which assist your approach put you in good position to be struck by lightning. This fire is not in my hands. You have this loving companion with you called God. You cannot do this by yourself.

You are taking on one of your purposes for being. Enjoy it.

One Power

Sunday Reading and Practice

The concept of one power is the basic teaching of spiritual science. It says that God is the only power and presence in existence. However, many metaphysicians so easily forget it. We are healing a sense of separation. It reminds us that God is an infinite presence. Now if something is infinite filling all space and time then where is there room for any other presence?

No longer should you place power in governments, companies, groups of people, or anything other than God. No longer should you stand near a person and attribute negative energy as emanating from that person. God is the only power and that power is good. Understand that God is good, but don't seek to judge things as good or bad. Don't move to judgment at all. Just call all of existence the one.

Recall that one of our purposes is to clean up our area of the pool. We can only do this through our thinking. Any actions we take follows from what we think and believe. If for some reason you are judging a person as being sourced in negative energy and you choose to believe this, you are adding to the dirt in the pool as opposed to accepting your purpose. Your purpose is to clean up mind. This is done by growing in your acceptance that God is all there is.

Many believe that through the obtaining of some person, place in life, or thing that they will reach true happiness. Some believe that through some change in their life happiness with come. I submit to you that true happiness and peace will only ground itself within you through the cleaning of your pool. Every time that you remove an erroneous thought from your mind either consciously or unconsciously you will experience a sense of joy. Every time something occurs within that removes any of the filth or erroneous judgments within consciousness a heightened sense of peace will occur within you. This is the only way to a lasting sense of peace and joy. Some of you may have heard that it is possible to be joyous most of the time and that it is natural. Cleaning of the pool is the way to this consistent peace and joy.

Have you ever spent significant time with a priest or with one of the holy men or women of the world? I recall spending some significant time with this holy man from Africa some years ago. Specifically recall the elevated sense of peace that he seemed to possess as he moved through his day. This man made the habit of keeping his attention on the God within him.

For example have you ever felt that high place after a church service? The real reason for your elevated feeling is due to your mind being on a quality or some truths about God. It takes you higher when the fog of the world is not upon you. Are you beginning to get it? This book is about cleaning up the fog within you. This writing will say this same thing in numerous ways. You must get to the place where you actually believe that GOD IS ALL THERE IS.

This is your ticket to absolute happiness and peace. Believe anything else and you are not judging righteously. We will deal with this specific topic of judgment later herein. For now please understand that unless you perceive the presence of God at all times, you are not judging righteously. The primary purpose of this book is to teach you this. This is how we return to the Creator's house. This is how the soul begins its journey back home.

Understand that you will also gain tremendous power through doing this spiritual work. Of course, this is a misnomer. You already have power. You just haven't learned how to direct it. Yet, I warn you that your real reason for doing this is because you love God. Some of the changes you may desire in your life may have caused you to find this writing. Yet it is suggested to you that the spirit within you loves its creator. This is truly why you have found this writing. Please try not to begin to look for the benefits of this work. Looking for benefits delays the process because the looking means you have doubts. You will then just grow the doubts. Trust God. Just do the work and stay inside yourself.

Genesis Support

It has been my pleasure to begin my study of the Bible with the understanding that many if not most of Bible stories are not intended to be taken literally. They are mostly allegories and parables that teach a cosmic event through the use of a story. Actually most cosmic events where God was creating can only be communicated through stories. Can you imagine another way of telling a cosmic event to the state of consciousness that existed with humans thousands of years ago? Grab the lesson. Do not get caught up in the story.

So God created man in is own image…

—Genesis 1:27

And the Lord God took the man, and put him into the garden of Eden to dress it and to keep it. And the Lord God commanded man, saying, Of every tree of the garden thou mayest eat. But of the tree of knowledge of good and evil, thou shalt not eat of it; for in the day that thou eatest thereof thou shalt surely die.

—Genesis 2:15-17

Genesis is the first book of the Bible. In the first reference we are being told that man is a spirit. If God is a spirit and we know this to be true, then something in its image is also a spirit. This suggestion here is that we had no human form at this time. Also understand that a spirit has no gender. God of course has no gender as well. So once again the people reading this who believe they are female (you are not female, you are still a spirit as are the males who think they are men). Lets' not get too sidetracked at this point.

In the second reference we are being told not to eat of a certain tree that would give us more knowledge. Now how can a tree give you knowledge? Remember this is a cosmic event being reduced to a simple story for a group of humans that were on the planet thousands of years ago. Since a spirit doesn't eat, what is the loving creator telling its creation?

God was telling its creation to watch its beliefs. God is saying: "don't believe that anything exist other than God or good." Of course, later in Genesis we learn that God's child did eat of the tree. The story also goes on to say that the humans (Adam and Eve) then noticed that they were naked. This only means that we began to notice bodies. Prior to the time we saw no bodies at all. Prior to that time all that we saw was

God and aspects of God. Of course the aspects that we saw are such things as joy, peace, and harmony. These are the things that are usually referred to as the eternal verities.

At the time that God's child began to see something other than God that was the time that is often referred to as the "fall". This was the time of our mind becoming split. This was the point of separation from heaven.

Now this initial set of meditations is seeking to take you back to what God originally told his creation in words that are a little more direct. Believe in God only. Ground yourself in the belief in one power and only one power and presence.

Since that time humans have kept their attention on the things of the outer. What was true then is true today. Whatever you put your attention on will grow in your life. Thus we humans have been growing our belief in these things other than God for some time now. I therefore give you this stern suggestion: Begin the journey back to God by seeking to believe that God is the only thing in existence. That within you and all around you is the presence of God.

The idea of one power does protect the mind. Imaginary figures can take the mind seemingly off base and cause such divergences. If imagined there really is nothing to protect. Many areas of this writing assist seeing properly. The mind must be allowed to diverge into the imagination at times to create true art. Yet one power allows one to come back to the loving embrace of the infinite.

Chapter Summary

In this chapter the following points have been made:
- God is the only power

- Keep attention on God or good
- Believe that the pool is clean by believing in good only
- Qualities such as peace, joy and harmony are qualities of good worthy of attention
- Joy and peace are a natural states and can be experienced more often through cleaning of your pool

Meditation Practice for Today

Dearest spirit, I ask today that you assist me in growing my belief in you as all that exist.

Take two deep breaths (slowly) and feel the breath each time as you do this.

I therefore say to myself:

- There is just one power (one breath).
- There is just one (breathe).
- One (breathe)

Now close your eyes and say the above three statements to yourself slowly and continuously for about three minutes. Don't concern yourself if you are not saying the three statements exactly as written above. Just ground yourself in the oneness of all being. Say the statements in your mind with your attention on your breathing as best you can.

After saying the above statements for three minutes, spend the following four minutes in the silence with your attention on your breathing as best you can.

As you get in bed tonight, say to yourself after a deep breath, "one power." Rest in this power that has protected you throughout the day and allow yourself to be at peace as you rest in God.

Affirmation: I live in the presence of God and God only. I am one.

Never Leave the Father's House

Monday Reading and Practice

A man had two sons. The younger son came to his father one day and said, "please give me what is mine." The father then gave this younger son what was to be his inheritance. The son took this money and went off into a foreign land. Here he lived high on the "hog" for awhile wasting his inheritance. I can imagine the young man going into a bar and saying "drinks are on me."

Finally the young man ran out of money. He didn't have food to eat. He went to a farmer and asked if he could feed the farmer's pigs for him. While doing this he became so hungry that he actually jumped into the pen with the pigs to wrestle food from the pigs.

Then the young man came to himself. He thought about the fact that his father had servants that were living better than this. He decided to return to his father's house and ask his father if he could work for him. Upon the return home, the son encountered the father in the fields. The father was overjoyed upon seeing his son. He ordered his servants to kill the fatted calf to prepare for a feast. The father took off his robe and placed it upon his son's shoulders. The father took the ring off his own finger and placed it upon the finger of the son.

During the feast the older son came back to the house. He asked the one of the servants why all the noise inside. The servant told him that his younger brother had returned home and the father had killed the fatted calf and thrown this feast. This older son decided not to enter the house.

Upon hearing of this the father came outside to speak to the older son. The father said that this older son should rejoice. His young brother was lost and has returned home. The son then said that he had never left the fathers side and the father had never killed the fatted calf so that he could celebrate with his friends. The father responded with "all that I have is thine.[5]"

Of course you recognize this story as the Prodigal Son story. It is one of the more famous parables told by Jesus in the Bible book of Luke. Notice that it suggest that the child left home and later starts a journey back home. This is exactly what this writing is suggesting to you. Return to your home in God. At least start your journey back by acknowledging that you are on a path.

Of course the father in the story is God. Let's call the father mind. The only thing mind has are thoughts. Therefore all the characters and all the happenings are occurring within mind. Likewise all the characters and happenings are thoughts. We can further state that all the thoughts then represent something like that described in the story. By the way, your life is the same. All the things that you look at are thoughts that have taken form. They all represent some aspect of your thought system.

The story begins with the younger son stating a desire to be given his inheritance. This can be likened to your decision to leave heaven. First of all why would someone who lives in heaven decide to leave heaven? Like many of us, we are never satisfied with what we have. For some reason there is this belief that the grass is greener on the other side. You are in heaven right now. Regardless of your circumstances you are in heaven. The way to improve your circumstances is to clean your area of the pool. Find your unclean thoughts and let them go. Your unclean thoughts are your belief in separation. They are your beliefs that something other than God exist. Sounds like the Sunday meditation doesn't it?

Notice that it took grave circumstances for the son to decide to return to his father. I am sure he noticed when his money began to run low. He had to actually jump into a pig pen to come to this realization. His pool had to become very dirty. In other words his thoughts had become full of mud. The pressure of his circumstances caused him to want to return home. Are there circumstances in your life right now that would cause you to want to return to heaven?

Note something about the father upon the son's return home. He did not scold him about the amount of money previously given to him. The father immediately began to give to the son. God has everything, why would God withhold? Your land or pool is of tremendous value. Just mine it by cleaning it. Just let God be good to you.

An important point here is that God is a being of unconditional love. God is not a trader. Many of us have grown up with the belief that we must give something to God to get something. This may be another of your erroneous beliefs. If it is, just let it go. You may want to consider if you have given qualities to God that God does not have. For example, I suggest that the human concept of "tough love" is not a God concept. This is a human concept we have created for a situation when a loving parent must scold a child or be lovingly "tough" in some way. Conceive of God as a being that is a gentle and generous love at all times and this takes God out of the human realm. God can be gentle and generous at all times because God is not human. God can teach you in loving and gentle ways because God is God.

We should also deal with the importance of the fathers statements to the older son at the end of the story. "All that I have is thine" means that the father has given himself to you. You are to maintain your awareness of this. Everywhere you are God is there also. Keep God on your mind. This is your source. As a child of the infinite, you cannot be happy unless you know of the immediacy of the God presence. This presence regardless of the gender you give it is your source. You cannot access this incredible power unless you know it is with you. You may see this similarity to the concept of practicing the presence suggested earlier.

Stay in the father's house. Remember that you are mind with incredible power at your doorstep. You are not a body. You are a state of awareness. Nothing can hurt a state of awareness. Decide to stay in heaven. Never leave the fathers house. This house is something you can carry with you wherever you go.

I recall one of my visits to the Wednesday night service at my church. The minister asked one of the congregants why they come on Wednesday nights. This person then stated that they get renewed vigor at midweek when they come to church.

You may decide to go to church to feel the renewed vigor. Yet if you remember that you are always in the father's house this will not be absolutely necessary. Church services bring forth strength in numbers that you may need. This strength in numbers is what my earthly father taught me as fellowship. There is nothing wrong with fellowship with persons of similar beliefs to strengthen your belief system. The world of beliefs that most of us grew up in must be let go of to accept a new belief system. We therefore accept all areas available to us to grow into another way of thinking.

This chapter is suggesting that you be willing to stay in the father's house. Stay in heaven. This was given to you at your creation. Never let it go.

Viewing the Self

Up to now it has been suggested to you that you are not a body. Yes, you are spirit. You might already understand that spirit has no counterpart in the world our eyes see. That means that spirit has no physical description other than its energy. Since energy is the ability to move things in the physical world, this is an acceptable description of the power of spirit in the physical world. Some call this energy vibration. Yet there is another way of viewing yourself. You are an idea in the mind of God. Now what kind of idea are you? You are the idea of perfect peace, perfect joy, and perfect love. Breathe into this thought for a moment (I am perfect peace, perfect joy and perfect love).

If you think about this you can now understand why you are still in heaven. What else is heaven, but perfect peace, perfect joy, and perfect love? Again we can see that we are one with our true environment. All you will ever be able to use to describe your true self will be concepts that are intangible. The energy behind an idea gives it the power to affect the physical world. However, you must first get an understanding of the idea that you are.

Your real existence is spirit (spirit = peace + joy + love). All spirits have the power of God at their disposal. This is because all spirits are one with God. The problem is that our minds have not been properly trained. For example, you are so powerful that nothing can come into your experience unless somehow you have asked for it. All the things in your experience are thoughts within you that have taken form. Therefore if you want your life to change, the only suggestion is to withdraw attention from outer things. The outer things tell you of a world of separate things. This is the lie being told by your five senses. Recall that clearing up untruths is equivalent to cleaning the pool.

Now you have been given a way of looking at yourself. Yet this description of spirit is one that has no counterpart in the physical world. There is a measure of how you can begin to see if you are progressing in your belief that you are a spirit. If you continue to find yourself in want for the things of this world of effects, you are still defining yourself as a body. This may seem to be a harsh measure, yet it is an accurate one. A true spirit wants for nothing because it knows that it has everything. My suggestion to you is that you begin to want only God and God's kingdom. Trust that all other needs will be taken care of without your being in want for them. The power of God will support you in this endeavor as long as you do your best to clean the pool.

Situations and circumstances will be created especially for you if you sincerely take on the task of cleaning your pool. Errors of mind will be brought to your awareness at the appropriate time. Be patient and be willing to live in truth. Live in heaven.

Now if you live in heaven is there anything wrong? The suggestion here is that you get into the habit of accepting that all is very well regardless of what your senses tell you. Initially this may sound unusual. Yet this chapter is telling you that you live in heaven. If heaven is at hand as Jesus suggested, then all is well. As you continue to clean your pool, you will begin to recognize this. A life other than the life of God (separation thinking) is something less than heaven.

Begin to trust that due to past thinking it is can be difficult to accept a new belief immediately. Especially this one that tells you that you are not a body without giving you a tangible definition of what you are. Therefore, you will only be able to measure your progress toward this suggested belief by your thinking. In other words, you may consciously believe that you know a thing, yet your actions and thoughts tell you the truth of what you really believe. If you want for the things of this world of effects you are still within believing that you are a body. Being in want itself is also unhealthy. Want really means that you do not have. Without working on it consciously, this work will cause you to grow and mysteriously your needs will be met. This writing is suggesting that how you see yourself is important. It is understood that seeing yourself as a spirit can be a challenge. Your desires tell you the truth of what you believe you are.

The Existence of Fear

Suppose you are operating in a world of fear. If you are, you are living within a lie. Remember God is all there is. Accept this fully and any fear that you are experiencing should disappear into the nothingness from which it came. You are in heaven right now. Just be willing to accept this. Your willingness is all that is needed. If feelings of fear do not immediately recede, be gentle with yourself. Seek to become aware of the specific area that seems to be causing concern within you. Then be willing to let whatever may happen just happen.

Another method is to find a quiet place and either aloud or in mind give your fears to God. Don't seek to fix anything. Just give all fears that come up to God and have faith that whatever occurs just occurs.

Often fear is a sense that a specific thing may not turn out as desired.

If for whatever reason the mind keeps focusing on a fear. Just be willing to become an observer of the mind. Don't fight with it. Observe the thoughts. See yourself as an observer. Courageously be willing to let whatever may happen. Trust that God is good. This is an area of your growth that God definitely has interest in.

In truth since God is all that there is there is no reason to operate in a state of fear. Of course since it is being mentioned here it is believed to be a state that many live in. Yet fear is the result of misplaced beliefs. There is never a good reason to live in a state of fear. Live in a state of love.

Defenselessness

Another area that should be given thought is the concept of defenselessness. Live in defenselessness. This means that you should not spend too much time seeking to protect yourself or anything that is dear to you. Seeking to protect yourself means that you believe that something is seeking to attack you. This is a very important concept. It is not what you think that is important. What is important is what you believe. If you spend too much time protecting yourself, your actual belief is that something is coming to get you. Clean your area of the pool by living undefended. There is nothing to be concerned about.

To practice living undefended, please stand up and stretch your arms out to the side. Close your eyes. Your arms and body should form a cross as you do this. Remember this as a model for how you live undefended. Your entire chest area is open and you are fully exposed to everything. Nothing is defending you as nothing is coming to get you. Visualize this as a way of living. You have nothing to fear.

A person's actions are based upon belief. You make a choice

because you believe something. Thoughts alone are not as important as beliefs. If you begin to notice beliefs you bring them to your conscious awareness. This is the first step in changing beliefs. If they are not in conscious awareness beliefs can drive your life without your knowing it. The work to be done based upon this writing are to help you become aware of your beliefs so that you can change them for your benefit. One of the benefits of meditation is its help in assisting one to be more aware of their own thoughts and beliefs.

One of the interesting things about Buddhist belief as I understand it is that there is not a deity in Buddhism. In other words there is no being called God. All is mind. Life is about gaining a better understanding of mind. Chanting is a way of the cessation of a roaming mind. It is very effective for this reason.

Chapter Summary
In this chapter you should remember the following:
- Make a commitment to return to the father's house by knowing you are already there
- Your are mind and all things in your life are thoughts that have taken form
- The response of God is always to give
- You have infinite power at your disposal
- Spirit is perfect peace, perfect joy, and perfect love which is your identity
- Fear can be conquered by taking belief away from it
- Live undefended

Today's Practice

The practice today is one where we remember that we never left the father's house. We are to remember that we have chosen to return home and are at home right now. God has prepared this home where all spirits like us live and some have preferred to call this home heaven. It really is not a place. We are so immersed within it as it is God itself and cannot be separate from it. Yes, we are one with God.

Beloved one, my request of you today is that you assist me in knowing that I live right now in heaven and that you, my source are always with me.

Begin this meditation by tensing up every muscle in your body. Start with you hands. Ball your hands up real tight. Now tighten up your arms. Extend this tightening to your abdomen by tightening up your abdominal muscles. Now tighten up your legs. Spend about twenty seconds to tighten up all the muscles in your body. Hold your breath while you do this.

Now let them go. Breathe deeply. Now spend three minutes telling yourself:

- I am in heaven right now (breathe).
- Heaven is my natural state (breathe).
- I am perfect peace, perfect joy, and perfect love (breathe).

These last four minutes of your meditation are to be in the silence giving your total attention to your breath. Note that some of the meditative phrases are stated in the first person. This is important for you. This helps with your ownership of them.

As with the practice noted earlier, every three hours you are remember that you are currently in heaven. Let nothing tell you otherwise today.

Affirmation: I am heaven and heaven is all I experience.

Now Is the Only Time That Is Real

Tuesday Reading and Practice

In the past we have seen many things and judged them as we have perceived. The sliver of time called the now has less judgment. This is because there is less baggage in the now. Suppose you moved each day and had to drag your belongings to a new station each day. This would be a challenge. We have seen homeless people who do this. Yet this is what you do when you carry the past along with you.

Now liken the past as a ball and chain. Why drag a ball and chain around? This is what the past is. It is heavy. It doesn't matter whether the past is good or bad. It is very heavy. It also carries some erroneous beliefs.

Once saw a film where brain activity was shown. Somehow this microscopic activity was recorded to show what happens when the brain is recording a new set of instructions. The brain actually builds something that looks like threads to other parts to assist its memory of using multiple muscle groups. For example, once you learn to walk the brain will record in a thread within itself with all the instructions you need to walk. In this way the brain is making itself more complex and remembering all the muscle groups to do a function.

There is a second central computer in the chest. This is the solar plexus. It is the part of the brain that monitors the functions that one does not consciously control. For example the solar plexus monitors functions like the heart and liver. You are unable to tell your heart to beat or tell you liver to function in one way. You are able to tell your hands to move and your body to run because here you are using the brain in your head.

The solar plexus is located behind the heart in an area called the heart cavity. It has one nerve that connects it to the brain. Without going too deeply into body chemistry and other body areas, understand that the solar plexus also has great connection to your endorphins that flow through the body. If you live in a state of fear and pressure, your body will continuously release endorphins that will cause you to prematurely age. Can you now see another reason why these practices will be so good for you? If you believe that you are constantly in the presence of divinity you should be relaxed.

If you are able to accept the value of the nervous system you could see that the central part of the feeling nature of the body is the solar plexus. Many have assumed this to be the heart due to the heart value in staying alive. The heart is the obvious noise maker within the body. It causes the heartbeat. Yet since it is a muscle, it doesn't control the feeling nature of the body. It just happens to be in the same body location as the solar plexus. The feeling nature is the solar plexus. This is where the nervous system is monitored.

How would you like to have all your nerves on the outside of your body? This is what you do when you think on the past too often. Liken it to keeping a rope that rings a loud bell in a public square. Would you like to leave your rope in right in front of everyone so anyone could "jerk your chain".

We won't belabor this point too long. We do use the body with breathing to get to the now, yet we are not of this world. We are spirit/mind. Staying in the now is the safest way of keeping life simple and living in faith. This is really the practice of faith. Your focus point is the now. The future is in God's hands. By the way, God can be trusted.

> The secret of success is nonattachment to results; doing your best at the moment, and letting the results take care of themselves[13].
>
> —J. Donald Walters

Suppose something happens to bring up one of your past issues. If this does happen you are to refuse to buy it. You have no issues. You are a perfect spirit. Remember all of your past was taken in when you thought you were a body. Now you know that you are a perfect spirit created by a perfect and loving God. Therefore if this thing happens just breathe through it. Just breathe. You may add to your strength by saying to yourself that you have no issues. Bring your attention back to the now.

There are times when it may appear that an issue is persistent. There may be something within that is seeking to come to your conscious awareness. In other words, there may be some good information within a persistent issue. Simply say to yourself "how should I understand this." Honestly desiring to understand is a key here.

One way of practicing living in the now is to take yourself to the now as often as you can. For example, suppose you are in a doctor's office and awaiting an appointment. Instead of picking up a magazine and keeping your mind busy, just take that opportunity to meditate. Bring your attention to your breath, close your eyes, intend to bring yourself to the now and just breathe. Take this opportunity as often as you can when you find yourself just waiting. A three minute meditation before picking up that magazine will be good for you.

This can happen in a supermarket while waiting in line or the many opportunities we get to just center ourselves. Actually the supermarket example is a good opportunity to bring up another point. Instead of getting impatient when a line is long in a supermarket or any retail line, use this time to meditate. Learn to meditate with your eyes open by just withdrawing your direct attention from things. You can do this by just relaxing and letting the happenings continue. Suppose someone near you complains that the supermarket line is long and that the management of the store needs to do something. Stay within. Don't agree that something is wrong. Agreeing that something is wrong is muddying the pool. Just smile and stay with your focus on the now. It will give you an opportunity to practice patience instead of feeling frustrated by a line and thinking thoughts that muddy the pool. Remember any feeling of frustration, anger or the like adds to the mud in your pool. Your purpose is to clean this pool.

Another view of this is the human condition that we always have better things to do than be where we are. This hurrying to get somewhere is an awful way of living. Being on your path brings forth patience. This is another measure that you are progressing.

Be gentle with the self. Don't expect perfection immediately. Just be willing to stay present and practice this. You will make mistakes, yet you will also improve daily with these practices as a way of life. You are cleaning the pool of mind. Frustration, impatience, and the like are choices that you make. Nothing can cause you to experience these emotions. Choose healthy emotions. Consciously choose to be at peace always by staying present.

Actually, the work that this writing is doing should be taking you to a point where you have less concern about the outside world. Your world is heaven. You stay in heaven by staying in the now and keeping your attention on that center within you. Only if you have experienced this in the past will you know what I am talking about. Or by beginning the work in this book you will eventually experience it. The best description I can give you of this practice is to be an observer. You are an observer of the happenings outside your body and an observer of the thoughts that go through your mind. You are not the thoughts nor are you the thinker. You are the observer of the thinker.

A simple direct way of stating this is the bible caution that one cannot serve two masters[16]. For me this created conflict. Choose God. Choose Love.

Now remember you are to find your source every three hours of each day. It is not critical to this process that you actually remember what the meditation is for that day while you are out and about. Just take a minute to remember God and bring yourself to a complete stop as best you can. Try not to judge your progress.

Picture yourself driving a car and coming to a stop sign about to make a right turn. Bring the car to a complete stop. Do not drift through the stop sign. This is how you are to do your one minute meditation. Be willing to bring yourself to a complete stop. Your mind doesn't have to become completely quiet and still. Just be willing to bring all your thoughts to your breath and relax. If things come up in your mind that is ok. Just give your complete thought to your breath as best you can.

Remember there is no wrong that you can do here. No one can ever do better than the best they can at that moment. Do not begin to see that thinker within as a problem that won't be still. Don't judge your thinker. Just do the best you can.

The following is an excerpt from A Course In Miracles textbook:

Everyone experiences fear. Yet it would take very little right thinking to realize why fear occurs. Few appreciate the real power of the mind, and no one remains fully aware of it all the time. However, if you hope to spare yourself from fear there are some things you must realize, and realize fully. The mind is very powerful, and never loses its creative force. It never sleeps. Every instant it is creating. It is hard to recognize that thought and belief combine into a power surge that can literally move mountains…. There are no idle thoughts. All thinking produces form at some level.

The suggestion here is to stay in the now away from thinking. Clearly there are times when you must allow the imagination to flow. Yet living in the now concentrating thought on the breath is a good practice.

Chapter Summary

In this chapter you are asked to recall the following:

- Desist from dragging the past around by living in the now
- Desist from allowing others to "jerk your chain" by staying present
- Faith is living in the now
- Bringing attention to some aspect of a present body action such as breathing may help bring one to the now
- Anger, frustration and the like add to the mud in the pool of mind

Practice of the Now

Take a few deep breaths and bring your full attention to the breathing points. This is either the nostrils or the abdomen. These focus points are what connect you to the now. As you breathe you cannot feel yesterday, nor can you feel tomorrow. As you breathe just seek to stay present. Now take your index finger of either hand and point straight down to the floor (this means be here, now). Use this exercise to remember the now.

Dearest one, my request of you today is that you assist me now and throughout this day to stay present.

Now spend three minutes telling yourself the following:

- Now is the only time that is real (breathe).
- Now is all that matters (breathe).
- I love it here in the now (breathe).

Give all your attention to your breathing as you continue saying this. You should spend about three minutes making the statements over and over. Now is the only time that is real. Now is all that matters. Then spend the last four minutes of your meditation in the silence.

Affirmation: I live here now.

FORGIVENESS

WEDNESDAY READING AND PRACTICE

Often forgiveness is something that is learned as letting go of a fault or a sin. However, this is not the definition we want to focus on. The world we live in that we have looked at all our lives is not the real world. The real world is the world of the soul. The world we have looked at is the world of illusion. Therefore everything that we have seen all of our lives has been the erroneous world. We can forgive anyone and everyone including ourselves because all that we have seen has never happened. Get this, all that we are seeing is not really happening because only that which is happening at the soul level is real.

The purpose in believing this is based upon the assumption that it is in the world of the soul where changes can be made. Seeking to change the outer world is less effective or only temporarily effective at best. Changing the world of your beliefs brings about more effective change.

Assume that God is good. Would God create the world that we now live in? God is too perfect to create such an imperfect world. The world we live in was created by a being that is best called "ego." The real world or the world of the soul is perfect. Within it everyone lives in perfect peace and enjoys the riches of a wonderful creation. This has been called heaven by many.

Heaven exist here and now. This is your true home. It is where the real you or the soul of you lives. It is not a place that you go to after the body dies. This is why Jesus states in the Bible that the kingdom of heaven is at hand[6]. By cleaning up your mind you restore yourself to a heavenly state. You are to live from here in a heavenly state. All five senses can experience and enjoy what the heart already knows. If you are willing to understand that the real you is the you that is a soul or spirit, you can then begin to experience the real world. You can then begin to live with your soul. You can begin to live in heaven.

The only real sin is to believe the world that your eyes see. It is a sin to have a split mind and believe that people and all things are separate. You stop sinning by accepting this as an untruth. You stop sinning by accepting that God created a perfect world called heaven that exist everywhere. This includes right where you are right now. All of creation is actually screaming out to you "See me as I am. See me as a whole and perfect spirit." If you choose to see anything else and call it the truth, you are sinning. Do not judge in this way.

You cannot help seeing these things. Yet you have a choice of believing them. I am simply asking you to have faith in a God that is perfect. A God that would not create a world like the one the news tells us that is happening. This three dimensional world is a lie. It is also the father of many other lies.

Are you beginning to get the picture that is being suggested? If our meditation on oneness is seeking to tell you that all is one, then what are your eyes seeing? Your eyes are seeing the erroneous world that your ego created. Your eyes are seeing the split world that they were made to see.

You enter heaven by accepting that soul is all that you are and all that really exist. The ego wants more money or a different or new mate or possibly a litany of things of the world of effects. This is not what your soul wants. The real you wants to unite the mind to know the truth about itself. This is why we are told to build treasures in heaven as opposed to on earth[7]. Your treasures are your accurate beliefs. I will now summarize what has been said in this chapter:

1. The real world is the world of the soul.

2. My five senses were not made to experience the world of the soul.

3. My real existence is right now in heaven. I am a soul in heaven now.

4. Choosing to mend the split in my mind I therefore accept that the world of the soul is the true world and everything I see as illusion.

5. The only true sin is to see the separation that seems to be everywhere and believe it is true.

Here you are given a choice. You may continue to chase the world's goods and side with the ego. Lets' not create an ego as a separate being. I am and you are ego as per previous beliefs. Now we seek to transcend this human self with new eyes and beliefs. You may choose to seek to heal your split mind and side with your creator. In my experience of years of siding with my ego, all I experienced was more pain and suffering. I will not claim to have had all my desires come to me. However, I can claim to be joyous and living a life in peace. I am also consciously on my path.

God created you with incredible powers that you have not learned to use. Everything that comes into your experience is something that you have created. Accept this. You are so powerful that nothing can come into your experience unless you at some level have asked for it.

I have been blessed to have been taught by a brilliant minister who created a model that list four stages of spiritual growth. If you still believe that things are coming from someplace other than yourself, you are in stage one which is the lowest and most painful stage. This is the stage of believing that you are a victim. A victim is one who believes that he/she has no control over life and circumstances and situations just occur randomly with no fault of those affected. All one does at this stage is struggle with conditions that seem to be worth fighting. Is it sensible to fight with yourself?

You are now asked to forgive all that you see. Call it illusion. There is great power in this. If you turn your attention from all that you see and begin to believe that heaven is all that exist you will begin to experience heaven on earth. You are now asked to begin to live from within. Breathe now and feel the truth. Feel the heaven within you. Live from this space and call this the truth. Peace, joy and love are the states of a heavenly mind.

Living from here all the errors that your erroneous mind has created will flee from you. Heaven will come to you. In the Bible there is the statement: "Be still and know that I am God.[8]" Feel the stillness within you and accept this as the only truth. From a period of living from the inner stillness or inner heaven, the outer world will then take the form of what is your truth.

The Holy Spirit

Some of you may be aware of this being God created called the Holy Spirit. This being is a spiritual being that God gave to you at the time of your creation to help you navigate your way through the world of illusion. You are asked to begin to ask this spiritual being for help with all your major decisions. Do not from here seek to rely on you own level of maturity. Having lived in the illusion so long you have no ability to make good decisions by yourself. You cannot make good decisions with a split mind. Use the Holy One as often as you can.

The Holy Spirit is a teacher. Some use other names for their spirit guide. My choice is just to name this guide the Holy Spirit. As everything in the spirit world, it is one with God. This being was created just prior to the fall or belief in a separate earth and heaven. The Holy Spirit was created to help you heal your split mind that believes it is separate from its creator. Use it for this purpose. You will need practice at doing this. The lessons of the Holy Spirit are gentle. Only your ego has those harsh lessons. Recall one power to stay in understanding one voice.

It has been my experience that the Holy Spirit answers sometimes with words and at other times with direct experiences. Be careful of a voice that promises things. This voice has rarely delivered for me. It may take some practice to learn of the different voices within you. Take the time to practice. Experiment with them. The Holy Spirit is very patient. The ego voice is not. Learn the ways of the Holy One within you. This is very personal and must be personally experienced. The Holy Spirit belongs to you and you belong to the Holy One. In Appendix II a few personal experiences of the Holy One are provided for you.

The Complete Breath

Another practice that is energetic and moves away from mental work alone is the complete breath. It is also a grounding technique. You do this by breathing slowly and easily. You are to expand your abdominal area first with air then raise your chest and expand this with air. Hold this breath for a count of two. Then exhale slowly. Repeat. You may want to watch the abdomen (belly) and chest to feel and see what is being done. Seek to exhale all your breath by bringing in the abdominal during exhalation.

This is a yoga technique and is to be done when starting your meditative period or anytime you want to experience the now and find more energy for whatever you do. Do this now for a few minutes if you are sitting in an upright chair. After practice it can be done in many positions. Some have noted that this is considered natural as the body breathes more deeply during sleep at times. The practice is to be done with breathing through the nostrils.

Chapter Summary

In this chapter you are asked to recall the following:
- Make forgiveness a part of your practice
- Forgiveness means that what our eyes see never happened
- The world of the soul is the real world
- Build a relationship with the Holy Spirit to get assistance with a split mind

Today's Practice

Your practice today moves you in a direction of forgiveness. This is one of the most powerful practices you will ever do. It helps you move toward the world God created.

Most beloved one, help me to live today in forgiveness of myself, everyone, and everything. Help me see or at least believe in the wholeness of all things that exist.

Your meditation for today is simply (note again the first person statements):

- I am willing to live in forgiveness
- I am willing to forgive myself

Willingness is key. Say this for the first three minutes of your meditation and use the last four minutes to just breathe and focus on your breath in silence.

Affirmation: I forgive myself and everyone around me.

THERE ARE NO LAWS BUT GOD'S

THURSDAY READING AND PRACTICE

Imagine a person we shall name as Harry who is fearful about air travel. For this reason Harry has decided never to get on an airplane. Some years ago Harry read about a plane crash where upon impact the jet fuel ignited and the resulting explosion burned the 500+ passengers to death. After reading these gory details, Harry decided never to get on an airplane again. He decided that plane travel is too dangerous.

Further suppose that Harry lives in New York and has decided to take a trip to Los Angeles. Harry decides to drive himself to Los Angeles from New York. Of course Harry could have taken a bus or train. Each of these methods would have kept him on the ground which is the deciding factor.

Most of us know that it is much safer statistically to fly the 3,000 mile trip than it is to drive. Yet Harry, due to his decision regarding plane travel has decided to drive. It will take Harry several days as opposed to the five hour nonstop flight time. There will also be much wear and tear on Harry's car as of course he will have to make another 3,000 mile trip on his return.

Harry has created a law within his mind. By this law Harry is unable to get on an airplane. Now this is an unusual way of looking at the concept of law, however please take a look at this. A law is a rule that seeks to inhibit action in some way. Doesn't Harry's law do the same thing?

This is an imaginary story, however consider the means under which Harry's law was created. He read a something that created a fear within him. He then made a decision based upon that fear. Now if we look at his decision regarding the trip to Los Angeles we can see that his law is putting him in danger. I once read that a car traveling between Los Angeles and New York will have 33 accidents before a plane will have one accident. Now at highway speeds, how many of those accidents will Harry survive? Thus, in terms of safety, Harry's law puts him more at risk.

The purpose of this story is to look at the concept of belief. Once a person accepts a belief, that belief becomes like a law to that person. It doesn't matter whether that belief has a fear behind it or not. Beliefs have that effect upon life. They either hinder life or broaden it. This story was created to show how a belief can hinder life. The purpose of this chapter is to introduce a belief that is to support broadening life.

The Law of God

The Law of God says that the only belief worth having is a belief in the support of the creator. This law is referring to God's love for its creations. This law supports you and me. Now you must accept this law and give less attention to the laws you made. Remember that through beliefs you create laws in your mind. This is where beautiful work can be done.

Another very simple statement of this law is as follows: "God loves and supports me." How much more simple can this be made. God loves and supports you. God is all around you. God is all there is. Since God is love this law is the law of love. It is magical and wonderful. As a child of God who loves its parent, you are to learn to fully love God as God loves you.

Law can also be understood as the way that things take form. An understanding is that some laws are physical, some are mental, some are made by humans, and finally there are laws of God. The word law is used here because it helps contain things.

For example, suppose there was a place where no human laws were made. The assumption is that anarchy would exist. Many of us have seen the old westerns where some of the western territories had not yet become states. While this was a part of human history, it is not to be used to guess at how societies would develop.

Recall the concept of the lawman. The sheriff or the marshal was charged with keeping some sense of order. Again the parallels are that people or laws maintain a place in order.

Consider how the planets circle the sun and how the sun circles the center of our galaxy. There is something that maintains this order such that the movement of these objects occur with a precise timing. The best clocks are not as precise. This is an example of law as a force that holds things in order. The planets are not colliding nor are we aware of other objects in outer space colliding. Haley's comet comes back into view of the earth at a certain time and this can be depended upon. It is in this way that it is suggested that we view the laws of God. They can be depended upon to complete their function. The function of the laws of God are to care for you. Isn't this beautiful? You have a law whose only purpose is to care for you.

Cause and Effect

Given a set of conditions, we should expect a consistent result. The confusion results because the conditions we are viewing are done so with the eyes. We should be careful not to create new laws in our minds by assuming that we can use scientific theories that only view outer conditions as the determinants of other outer conditions.

This writing is suggesting that inner conditions create the outer. Using the view of outer events solely to suggest cause is flawed. Science uses this method as a matter of requirement because commonly science does not recognize the soul or the power of thought. This is the simple statement of cause and effect. Since you cannot see the inner, how can you expect a consistent outer result?

This writing is not intended to criticize the progression of science. We are talking about personal spiritual growth here. Science has a place and must be respected. However more information will not heal you or our planet. Reliance on God will.

If you for example believe in the power of germs and viruses you can create another law with this belief. Tying this concept to living undefended is where you do not seek to constantly keep things clean because of your belief in germs. There is a medical term for those who constantly wash their hands and get very afraid during the so called flu season. You are to keep your body clean and your surroundings as well. Yet be careful of becoming overly cautious about germs. There is a level of sanitation that is perfect for you as a spiritual being.

There are physical laws that you maintain a healthy respect for. Actually the so called physical laws are lesser laws because you are not a physical being. You are spirit. You can rise above these lesser laws by learning the truth and living in truth.

A Place for Your Will

Humans have attempted to will a good life into place for many years. Willing something that is already in place is without merit. Nothing of permanence occurs. The creations of God unlike the human creations have tremendous power behind them. They do not need your help.

The practices taught in this book suggest a perfect place for the will. Will yourself to do the practices. Will yourself to believe that you are progressing spiritually. Will yourself to believe that God is all there is. Will yourself to stop believing the things your senses try to tell you. Will yourself to believe that God is good and all that God created is good. Use your personal will and personal charisma with regard to yourself and others to bring a practice into place. Yet, do not will yourself to make life good. Life is already good. Yet this may be below the level of your senses. Remember the place for your will and use it appropriately.

The laws of God are simple and do not bring any complexity at all. They are one. God is the one. Ask any question and the answer is the same. God is the one answer. This may be difficult for some minds to grasp initially. It requires a progression from the other sets of laws that are numerous and complex. However accept that God is the one answer and you have entered a realm that is above all the other laws. You may not have transcended the other laws, but you have entered a new door.

This is the highest law. It works above all the other laws. It requires the simple mind of someone who is willing. The brilliant mind of the scientist can also see this. Here both come together to know that God is good. The law of good is all that matters. You will never learn the laws of God from a book, nor deep meditation. These help and are part of the process. A simple faith is all that is needed. With simplicity we see that anyone can do this.

Mother Teresa, Martin Luther King, and Mahatma Ghandi are three people who let a simple faith allow them to make significant contributions to society. Most importantly they grew to astounding heights spiritually through a love each had for their creator. Learn to say this to yourself often. There are no laws but God's. Say it when things are going good. Say it when things appear otherwise. There are no laws but God's. This is the placing of your reliance upon the things you do not see or understand. There are no laws but God's.

Can you see how simple faith is? Are you beginning to understand how powerful a simple faith is? Leave the complexities of the world you used to live in alone. Live in the simple and beautiful world that God created. Live in the world of soul. Live in heaven. There are no laws but God's.

The purpose of this chapter is to begin to take your mind away from other beliefs that you may have. It strengthens the mind and leaves it free of erroneous beliefs. Your creator did not create you to believe in the numerous sets of laws that are so complex. These laws have no effect upon one who has accepted the law of good. The law of God is the law of good. A mind that is too logical and wants to fully understand cannot conceive of infinity. The small cannot contain the infinite. Open up mentally and let this principle find its place within you.

A miracle state of consciousness is now being built within you. You are to grow confidence in yourself and truth. Sometimes your actions may not be popular. You are not entering a popularity contest. Things are not small or big in this way of thinking. Time of growing such a mind has no effect either. Skip many steps with letting the love of God grow in you. Love does not see size. Is a Galaxy more important to God than you? God sees all of this with an equanimity.

A Word About Self Love

While this writing is suggesting that you are mind there is another use we can make for the body. Suppose you want to do something like lose weight. Many have thought that if they make certain body changes it will improve self love. This writing is suggesting the opposite. Accepting the body as it is is an improvement in self love. Yet since the body is not our true identity the appearance of it really doesn't matter. Put nothing into the future. If you can accept the body now as it is, you are in a better position at improving self love. You will also be in a better position toward reaching any body goal such as losing weight.

Recall that the purposes of this writing is to remove the sense of separation. It is also premised upon the belief that removing this error takes care of everything. Therefore if for example you have a body goal that is OK. Yet remember to begin to define yourself properly. Your beliefs are what we are working on. The pool is clearing up.

Chapter Summary

You are asked to recall the following from this chapter:
- Beliefs create mental laws in the mind
- Mental laws either create freedom or they create limits
- The law of God is simple and the only one you want to believe in
- Use the will appropriately
- Size does not matter
- Self love improves by accepting yourself now

Practice for Today

Our practice today has the purpose of erasing from our minds all the erroneous beliefs that have us believing in other causes. The good law of God is the only cause.

Beloved one, assist me today in letting all beliefs in laws other that the one you created go from me.

Say for three minutes:

- There are no laws but God's (breathe)
- I love God (breathe)

Then for the following four minutes meditate on the breath with attention on the breath in silence. Remember to bring your attention to your center every three hours.

It should also be noted here that growing a stronger love for God here increases your self love. Remember you are one with God. Raise you hand if you want to love yourself more (I assume that this is a universal desire). By the way, smile.

Affirmation: I love God as myself.

Gratitude

Friday Reading and Practice

Hopefully you have come to understand something by now. Your true power is that of your attention. Whatever you give your attention to will grow in your life. Whatever you take your attention away from will wither and decrease from your life. These meditations in this book are seeking to assist you in focusing your attention only on that which is real. Keep your attention on the God within. Don't live in that world of your creation (ego creation) as it will only hurt you. Live in the world that your creator created and you will find the only world acceptable to a creation of God.

My spiritual practices started some years ago reading a book called The Science of Mind[9]. In this book the author says the same thing in another manner. It says that if you can take your attention off your problems your problems will grow feet and run from you. Many do the opposite. They try to solve problems. So what happens after solving a problem? Another is created. It is really the same problem in another form. Have you lived long enough to notice this? A split mind is your only problem.

You are not a problem solving machine. You can spend you whole life seeking to solve your problems or you can just begin to gain control of your attention and watch your problems disappear.

That which you appreciate appreciates. Remember this. Now there is one thing that you really want to grow in your life. God. Yes, you can increase the level of God and good in your life by consciously appreciating God. But, what is God. God is all there is. Therefore you are to appreciate every aspect of your life. You are to be thankful for the presence of God in your life.

> "We should be grateful. It is an important social grace. But even more, it is a requisite for high-level wellness[14]."
> —Dr. Eric Butterworth

Yes, without an attitude of gratitude it is difficult to experience true wellness. Lets look at the opposite for a moment. Suppose you know someone who goes around complaining all the time. What will the universe give that person? Well, the universe will generally give that person more to complain about. Do you want more to complain about? Of course that answer is obvious.

However, this is a good point to look at a related matter. Should you tell that person to stop complaining? Should you become the answer man/woman for others that you meet because you are spiritually developed? This answer is no. Please look at this carefully. If you start advising others you are in effect saying that the person you are advising is not the presence of God. Even if you are doing it with the intention of helping someone you must be careful here. Your primary task is cleaning the pool. Cleaning the pool means that everything and everyone you see is the presence of God. Giving advice is saying in effect that this person that stands before you needs your words and advice because they are not the presence of God. Stop it! Cease and desist! Notice that we are becoming aware of what we really believe by our actions as opposed to what we say we believe.

The most powerful practice you can do at these times is to call forth within this person the presence of God. Say nothing. Within yourself just say: "I accept that God is right where you are." Then within yourself become grateful because you caught yourself sinning and chose not to sin by not believing in error.

Of course it is not suggested that you never advise anyone. There may be times when it is helpful. It is especially helpful if the person ask for your advice. Most if not all other times you are to call forth (in silence) the God within that person. The true power of this practice is that on the inner plane you more easily see yourself as God if you can see it in others.

Please do not belittle this practice of gratitude. Jesus made the statement: "for he that hath, to him shall be given; and he that hath not, from him shall be taken that which he hath.[15]"

It may seem that a spiritual law that suggest the importance of having as a bridge to more is unfair. It is just leading one to a set of beliefs. If you really believe that you are poor, that is your ticket to permanent poverty. Begin a practice of gratitude for what you have. From here you will experience having more.

View yourself a spirit and let the laws of God begin to lift you without much effort at all. You don't need to chase the world of effects to enjoy life. Appreciate that heaven is where you are and let the stronger laws of spirit support you. As you learn and begin to believe truths about yourself and eliminate your erroneous beliefs, the truths will take care of the body and all of your affairs. Just let the truth be so.

Subtle Spiritual Power

The reminder is to be gentle with yourself. Use balance in your way of living to ease into the life as a spirit. A story to illustrate easing into the life of as a spirit is useful here.

One of my ministries at my church is the prayer ministry. I sit in a room and receive calls from all over the world. On one occasion a person called and mentioned that she was a recovering alcoholic. This person told me that her life had gotten so busy that she felt overwhelmed. She then mentioned that she often found life easier when she balanced her life with the twelve step program. Alcohol was no longer a problem in her life, but when she spent less time with the spiritual practices of the twelve step program, she felt that her life would just fall apart. Even though the spiritual practices of this program added more work to her life, she was beginning to notice that they seemed also to hold her life together.

In my view this person was beginning to notice the subtle power of spiritual practices. If these practices just keep your mind at peace, a person usually is able to handle life more easily operating from a peaceful mind. Yet my suggestion to you is that these practices do more than just make you feel better. If you initially give some time to spiritual practices they should bring you to a more peaceful state of existence. Yet, this writing is saying that truths in your mind do a great deal more. They are causative factors to the only life worth living. Truths within you eventually lift you into the life of God. Therefore be grateful that you are on a path to living in a world of truth.

The awareness here is that it is normal in western society to initially see spiritual practices as more work. The standard world does not recognize that which they do not see. Actually certain ways of living need not even be called religious or spiritual. The point is that meditative practices and living in a world that the eyes do not see may seem difficult initially. Let these practices prove themselves to you. Make it a habit to say thank you more often both within silently and without. On occasion take the time to list the things you are grateful for. Specifically, having a journal that you use to list the things that you are grateful for is suggested. Use your journal to also begin to list the truths that you are learning about. Take the time to journal. You will be glad that you did. I have been journaling for many years and I expect to do so forever. Gratitude practices alone will serve you well.

Chapter Summary

The ideas to remember for this chapter are as follows:

- Live in gratitude
- Become aware of where you place your attention
- What you appreciate appreciates
- Be careful about giving advice
- Learn to trust the power of truth
- Take the time to journal

Gratitude Practice

Today you are to practice begin grateful. As a being that creates where attention is placed it should be easy to see the value in this meditation. You must be grateful.

Holy one, I ask today that you assist me in being grateful for just having you in my life.

Start by putting both hands over your heart. Feel your heart beating for about thirty seconds. Now say to yourself:

- I am grateful for God being in my life
- I am grateful for God

Spend the first three minutes saying these words to yourself with your attention on your breath. Spend the next four minutes with your attention totally on your breath (as best you can).

Affirmation: I am grateful for myself and all that I am.

Help Your Sister to Heaven

Saturday Reading and Practice

This portion of the writing will now begin to refer to beings as if they were female. This is done for simplicity sake. The important thing to remember is that you can increase your spiritual growth immensely if you are willing to assist another. In fact you do not have a choice. Since reality is a seamless space, there really is nothing separating you from another. In other words, all that there is is you. If you help your sister you help yourself.

Have you ever done volunteer work and had that wonderful feeling of having done something without anything in it for you? This is what you do when you help your sister go to heaven.

Where is heaven? You are there right now. Heaven is all there is. It is not a place that you go to when you die. The truth is that you will never die. How can a spirit die? That body that you believe you are strongly attached to will one day end. Yet, you will never die. Actually, if you begin to believe this your body will actually get younger. It still won't last forever. Yet it will be more vibrant if you begin to properly define yourself, your sister, and your source.

God really has only one child. That one child is the soul. We all have the same soul. In truth, a thought does not have a gender. Unfortunately that child one day decided to create things. Those things caused a perceived separation in mind. Now we are on a great adventure to bring the mind back to its oneness.

The one child God created can be called the Christ. Yes, you are the Christ. You are the only child of God. This is what Jesus did. He realized that God had only one child and he chose to become that child. Be willing to become the Christ. Be willing to become the only child of God. You then unify your mind with the one mind. You then become the powerful being that your creator created.

If you define yourself properly, what is it that you could possibly want? Nothing. You want for nothing. Suppose you believe something is missing in your life. Well, you are perceiving incorrectly. You may want to watch your thoughts. You can see your progression toward correct thinking if you do this. The want for things of this world means that you think that you are a body. This body thinking must be given up. It is a lie that weakens your progression.

You are a perfect creation of the creator of perfection. Of course God is the creator of perfection. Since you are God's creation and we have defined God as the creator of perfection, what are you? Obviously you are nothing more than a perfect creation. You must begin to see yourself that way. This thinking will serve you well.

What does this mean? Well, it means that you have never done a single thing wrong. You are not a body, you are a soul. I use the word soul and spirit or each with the same meaning. It is for this reason you can unload all inner guilt that you may be carrying. See yourself and your sister as innocent.

Understand that you can be God's only child in spirit only. Ten thousand people can claim this at the same time and it will be true. This

I believe is one of the meditations of Jesus. God's only child can be named Christ. Let this Christ presence take over your life. Let it teach you how to be the Christ. Though you are here in the presence of all power, this requires a humility of you. Though you are the Christ, you don't know how to be it. The Christ presence is alive as God's only creation. It will come to meet you where you are and teach you how to be the Christ. I offer to you the definition of The Christ from the Science of Mind Textbook[9]:

> Christ, The; The Word of God manifest in and through man. In a liberal sense, the Christ means the Entire Manifestation of God and is, therefore, the Second Person of the Trinity. Christ is Universal Idea, and each one "puts on the Christ" to the degree that he surrenders a limited sense of Life to the Divine Realization of wholeness and unity with Good, Spirit, God.

Many have the habit of calling Jesus by the name Jesus Christ as if his last name is Christ. Jesus became the Christ. In the book of Matthew Jesus refers to himself as Jesus the Christ[10]. This writing is suggesting that you do the same. Be willing to become the Christ. Can you now see what happens when you begin to define yourself as an aspect of the whole? You give up any sense of a separate self. You are to surrender your ego which is that separate self.

The Birth

Another way of looking at this concept of rebirth has been given you. You are a mother carrying the Christ child. This child is you. You are to give birth to this child. You are to be born again by giving birth to a new you. This becomes your new life and the only life worth living.

Now do you understand what a "born again Christian" is? Being baptized and trying to be good alone will not cut it. Becoming a different thought is a path. Loving your sister as yourself is a path.

Now you help your sister by seeing her the same as you see yourself. Yes, everyone you see is the Christ as well. You are not to go around telling others this. You are simply to say this in your mind when someone does something or says something that causes you to see or believe otherwise. You accelerate your own spiritual growth by calling all beings your sister.

Chapter Summary

The important points of this chapter are as follows:
- Be willing to see your sister properly
- See yourself properly as well by maintaining awareness of your spiritual nature
- God has one child and you are that child
- You are willing to learn to become God's child
- Give birth to the Christ child

Practice

Some may have given Jesus the title of the only son of God. Son simply means created life of God. Jesus simply chose to become God's only created life, or God's only son. He merged his mind with the mind of his spirit so that the split in his mind disappeared. In other words, he gave up his ego, which is the giving up of any sense of separation from the whole.

Beloved one, teach me to see myself correctly. Teach me to see myself as a soul, the child of my creator.

Your words for meditation today are as follows:
- I am the Christ (breathe).
- I am the whole child of God (breathe).
- I am at peace (breathe).

Again the importance of the first person (I am) statements are brought out. Breathe deeply and slowly after each of these statements. Now close your eyes and continue.

Again, use the first three minutes to make the statements continuously to yourself. Then spend the balance of the four minutes in the silence giving your total attention to your breath.

Affirmation: I am a wonderful peace.

In Conclusion

Several years ago I returned home to Chicago to assist my family during one of the difficult times of our lives. The day I arrived and entered my mom's home someone was cleaning for her. Actually there were two ladies in the house that I had not seen previously. One was wiping the baseboards near the floor. Another was vacuuming in the living room.

I later learned that these were ladies from the church and they were assisting my mother. That evening someone arrived with a pot full of a stew and some chicken. This was to be the evening meal for our family. Again someone from the church had decided that it was necessary to save us the trouble of having to purchase or prepare the evening meal.

Several days earlier my earthly father had made his transition and each day someone from his church was doing something to help the family through this period of our lives. My father had been a Jehovah Witness and was one of the elders of this particular group.

At the time of his memorial service it seemed that there were hundreds of people that were in attendance. It took place at a Witness Hall in Chicago. Our family sat at the front of the room and I remember very little of what took place. I do recall at some point requesting that I be given a few minutes to speak to the group. A little later someone approached me and said that it was ok for me to speak for a few minutes. As I approached the stand in the pulpit I was looking at the audience in wonder. They were varied, but beautiful in every respect. For a few seconds my mind began to focus on individuals and I was surprised at the number of people that were familiar to me.

My words were short and were specific to a state of gratitude for all the gifts that many had poured out to my family. The house cleanings that were continuing as well as the food and most importantly the outpouring of love that I felt from the many who had taken the mantle of serving my family at this time. All of this was a surprise as I had never embraced my father's religion nor had I known of the breadth of his ministry.

It was later reported to me that this church had never allowed someone who was not a member of their faith to approach their pulpit. Simply because I was the son of Albert Collins I was allowed to speak to the group. Admittedly, this outpouring continues years later because of the work of my father. My mother continues to attend some of their services and she has a ministry as well, however my father gets more credit because he was the person who reached to title of elder of the church and often spoke quite eloquently to the congregation.

The only life worth living is about a conversation I had with my father that was later explained to me in more detail by my mother. My father had once said to me that his life would not be worth anything if not for his ministry. At the time I was a little disappointed as my father had previously told me that he was very proud of having raised five children from what was actually ghetto beginnings and all of us had done well in our lives. My mother explained to me that though my father was proud of his children, his ministry had done something more for him. His ministry had assisted him in getting rid of a personal selfishness and he had become a servant to humanity through his love for God. I was away at college when my father started his ministry so I was not aware of the depth of his work.

I now view my fathers statement regarding his life differently. I view it as my father actually giving up to a large degree his sense of separation through his love for God. My fathers teaching would never suggest anything like this due to their beliefs. Yet this is the whole premise upon which this writing is based. The only life worth living is attained through moving closer to God. My preference is to state it as giving up the sense of separation.

Somewhere during my practice I actually fell in love with God. Through this love my life seems to have a different dimension to it. It is a life wherein a purposeful life of giving and playing are objectives. The broad expanse of such a life has no limits because it is a life wherein I have chosen to allow God to take the helm. In my experience either God was at the helm or my ego was at the helm. In my mind these are the only choices. My life has had challenges and there has been times of despair. Yet this life bears witness to the power of God and the love that God has for creation. Since God has taken the helm, my life and my persona have begun to reflect the qualities of God.

It is important to note that this higher standard may not be popular. For example I remember coming across a bumper sticker that suggested that the most exceptional women that have walked our planet were not nice ladies. Add what you will to this statement. The crux of this is that you may not immediately or ever become well known or mainstream if God is truly at the helm. However with God at the helm life will take off in ways you may not have ever imagined.

Note that several of the meditations of this writing suggest that something is being asked to help you with seeing in a certain way. Most of us have been living within our egos so long that we need to ask for this help. It means that until more experience is gained with being a spirit, the norm is to operate as an ego. No criticism here, just an observation from experience. Certainly this was my personal experience.

There are some things that begin to happen once God takes the helm. Understand that this God does not take the helm of your life unless you allow it in some way. One thing is that you may be unsure of exactly where you plan to go with your life. Yet, that which is in control does know. In particular you may specifically tell God in whatever way you can that you aren't sure where you want to go, yet you do have the faith and trust in God that all will always be well with you. Living in the now sometimes feels this uncertain. Yet if heaven is remembered, the recollection that all is well is remembered as well. At some point, personal conviction becomes known and specific direction takes place.

Another example of this is something I studied while involved in a teacher training while attending a university. This particular class had begun to study the gifted child. In particular I remember that the definition of gifted suggested that a child is not gifted unless he/she gives the gifts away. Prior to this time I had focused on the intelligence of a person who was considered gifted. This definition focuses on the giving nature of the child. If the child does not at some point begin to give their gifts away they are not considered gifted.

I am not suggesting that you look for places to give to make your life work. These opportunities will either come or they have already come. Keep the thought in your mind that God is not a trader. Note that I am saying here that some level of spiritual practice must continue as long as you are on the planet.

That ego within may immediately complain about this. It may complain if you are used to being very busy and stillness practice is not the norm. Another term for this is mindfulness practice. Be confident that if you do this work and give up being a body the ego will not have a home. Your thoughts and body are all that this being has. Remember that only your thoughts keep it alive and calling yourself a body gives it a home. Be willing to see yourself as something other than a body. Love the body and care for it. Just don't limit yourself to it.

There will be some areas you may not fully understand. This is ok. It calls upon a quality God gave you at creation. You call on your faith and trust that all that needs to be revealed is being revealed. Please don't play the ego game that you must understand everything. I have not spent a great deal of time discussing the ego because there is a lot of literature about this. As well, the chapter on one power suggest that the ego does not exist. At minimum it is a symbol of a separated self. This writing is only pointing you back to yourself. It is not asking that you drink poisoned soda (smile). In other words there is no cause for fear here.

Hopefully you now understand why this book is so entitled. If you take on the task of clearing up the errors in your mind you will definitely experience the only life worth living. My suggestion is that you will be healthier and a happier being. The author can certainly claim that spiritual practice has brought a level of physical health not experienced previously.

I say this because prior to beginning a meditative practice I was plagued with various illnesses. They were not serious, however I had a bad habit of catching influenza once or twice a year. Influenza is very painful with the high fevers and chills resulting from this condition.

However since beginning a meditative practice I rarely get a cold and rarely suffer with that influenza which had plagued me most of my life. Admittedly, I did not notice these benefits of spiritual practice immediately. They just happened and are the result of living in peace. This is being mentioned to suggest some reasons to persist in your practice, however be careful approaching God or doing this work because you may want something. This "wanting" can impede progress. Do this work because you want a closer relationship with your maker or because you want to grow spiritually. Healing the sense of separation means the same as growing spiritually. Just awaken.

I continue my spiritual practice because I have fallen in love with my creator. My original start to this work was for other reasons. That does not matter now. It is also my belief that this is something my creator desires of me. My reliance is from the statement in Matthew when Jesus suggested the commandment to "Love God with all your might and love your neighbor as yourself[3]".

It has also been my experience that the person who shows up when I am consistently practicing is a person in human form that I find more able to love and be loved. This is my view anyway. On occasion during my meditations an experience occurs that is almost difficult to describe. My best explanation is a feeling of complete release and indescribable bliss. This experience itself is worth its weight in gold. Yet, this alone is not why I persist in my practice.

There have been points in this writing that have referred to my life or your life. Admittedly these terms are errors themselves. Once the work of healing the sense of separation begins you must figuratively jumps into the spiritual soup called God and acknowledge that there is really only one life. That life is the life of God. That life is good.

Belief in separation is the only thing that is cause of this sense of separation.

In the Bible there is a place where we are told to "hate our life[12]." Of course you should not hate your life, but you are being asked to give up the concept of having a separate life. Remember from the first chapter of this writing, it is the view of separation that is the only cause of a life of problems. From this simple view of that phrase "hate" it can be seen why it is important to read spiritual literature figuratively as opposed to literally. Give up your old life. Give up an outdated way of thinking. Become one with your creator in your beliefs.

Only you can let God define for you what is the only life worth living. Only you can surrender your own beliefs and let something that is the creator of all to complete you or allow you to see what is truth. Only you can take on the task of cleaning the pool of mind and do so in a gentle manner with yourself to continually affirm your self love. The choices are simple again. Serve God or something else. Become one with God or stay with your current beliefs about what you are. There is great power in knowing self. The mystics throughout the ages have taught this.

Parental Responsibilities

After over fifty years of being in the presence of children and endeavoring to maintain a childhood my entire life, I would be remiss if I did not add words for parents. This is an easy, but can be a new decision for parents. We as parents love our children and sometimes wonder about where they are going. Children are born with an innate ability to seek freedom. The wonder and risk seem to be without end. We then again enter the area where God and our trust that God maintains this kingdom is reviewed. Our children roam free to explore because they are still in the house of their creator like us. They are God's children as well. Trust that God and the child know this.

A parental responsibility is to allow children to explore themselves without parental fears. Fears are not things we want to pass down. God knows nothing of fear. God knows nothing of needing to protect anything. These are recognized as beliefs. We as parents have a responsibility to let God come out of the children. Education means that they were born with innate abilities. Parents can allow these abilities to flourish by standing aside at times. Please do not use love as an excuse to smother your children. A love that trust so wholly is understood by God.

Living on purpose requires that I allow my children to explore with the awareness that I am with them as well. My children saw a father who prayed often. Journaling has always been a part of my practice. Many sing, some dance, others write jokes. In the appendix is an example of an appropriately worded devotional essay. Hopefully you will enjoy it as much as I have.

Personally, I have this vision that a day will come when spiritual practice will be more commonplace and entire societies will be consciously guided by this incredible presence I have come to know as God. For God alone can teach us to truly love one another.

My prayer for you my beloved is that you find reasons to persist in your practice and prepare that place for God to descend upon you. Of course this is done by your acceptance of good or God as the only truth. In that place you and God merge with all. May you continue to broaden the numbers and depth of those who love you as well as those you love.

Peace and Blessings.

Author Biography

Gerald Collins is a Religious Science Practitioner at the Agape International Center in Culver City, California. Dr. Michael Bernard Beckwith, the founder and spiritual leader of Agape taught Gerald Collins as his minister and classroom teacher. Gerald has been an active practitioner since 1997 and a member of Agape since 1993. Mr. Collins has spent over 15 years teaching spiritual science and spiritual principles to children in church and has been an assistant teacher in the adult school. Through teaching children he found ways to simplify teaching complex spiritual principles. His career has been in teaching and financial management since 1976. He is a Certified Public Accountant and has a masters' degree in finance. Mr. Collins has written for a children's magazine and has been a writer for Innervisions, an Agape publication since 1997. He is an avid reader and has studied many of the mystics who have lived on our planet. This study of mysticism is believed to have had a great impact upon Gerald's belief system.

NOTES

1. Matthew 6:33
2. Luke 17:21
3. Mark 12:31
4. Matthew 17:20
5. Luke 15:31
6. Luke 17:21
7. Matthew 6:20
8. Psalms 46:10
9. Science of Mind Textbook, Devorss Publications
10. Matthew 16:20
11. Closer Is He Than Breathing, Alfred Tennyson
12. Luke 14:26
13. The Corporate Mystic, Bantam Books
14. Spiritual Economics, Eric Butterworth, Unity Press
15. Mark 4:25
16. Matthew 6:24
17. Page 31, A Course in Miracles, Published by the Foundation for Inner Peace

APPENDIX I

Excerpt from InnerVisions January, 2009
By Jennifer Hadley (www.jenniferhadley.com)
Here I AM, Take Me

For many years I was in dialogue with the Presence about my devotion. I had reached a point where I was headed toward my entering the Practitioner training and I was living mostly in alignment with Spirit—about 80%. I thought I was doing pretty good. I only needed 20% of my time and energy to hold in reserve in case I needed to be judgmental, impatient, and unkind or just lapse into some debauchery. I thought I was doing pretty good. 80% is way more than half—it's more than three quarters!

A year later I found myself back at the bargaining table. I made an offer that I thought was more than generous. I told God "take 90%", it's yours. All I needed was 10%—a little piece of land where I could have some shame and blame and whatever else I needed to get along and still be me. Honestly, I thought God ought to be satisfied with that.

Six months later I was back at the table. "95%—that's my best offer", I remarked. I needed only a tiny space where I could still recognize myself as the irritable, opinionated, knucklehead I knew myself to be.

Soon I realized that I could never be happy until I turned my whole life over. Whole Soul Devotion was all that would satisfy this hunger and thirst. There was nothing about me, no matter what I did, that God would reject, so why hold back? It was about my willingness. I could never be wholly devoted while the ego's craziness was dissolving. I did not have to wait until I was "without sin." Immediately I wanted to give all to the all. In my heart, I fell to my knees so gratefully and declared: "Here I AM, Lord. Come and take me. Let not another minute go by. Take me, I'm yours."

Appendix II

Living with the Holy Spirit

Purposefully, little was said about the Holy Spirit. The reason is because it is so personal. If too many examples are given, you might begin to limit this being. It knows everything about you. Actually, it knows you better than you know you. If you recall the trinity as God, Son, and Holy Spirit you will understand the importance of this being. These three are the only beings in existence. You are the son and the Holy Spirit is your guide. Below are several statements that were made to me by the Holy One:

"Dear Gerald. You cannot possibly love yourself as much as I love you. Please let me just love you."

"I have no ability to separate myself from you."

"Bring any perceived problem to me. I will answer."

"You are important to me."

"I am wise. I am infinitely wise."